I0796856

I LOVE YOU MOM

AND HERE'S WHY

This book was made for you with love by:

Mom,

WHEN I LOOK BACK ON THE YEARS WE'VE SPENT TOGETHER, I SEE THE VERY BEST BITS OF MY LIFE.

LIKE A HOME MOVIE ON FAST FORWARD, I CAN SEE THE MANY PHASES WE'VE BEEN THROUGH, THE MILESTONES WE'VE CELEBRATED, AND THE DINNERS WE'VE SHARED. I CAN HIT REWIND ON THE UPS AND DOWNS, THE SILLY TIMES, AND THE FORMATIVE MOMENTS. I CAN PAUSE TO REFLECT ON THE EVOLUTION WE'VE BOTH EXPERIENCED AS WE'VE GROWN OLDER, GROWN WISER, AND GROWN OUR RELATIONSHIP INTO SOMETHING NEW.

YOU'VE BEEN THERE FOR IT ALL, BUT NOW I WANT TO SHOW YOU THE FULL STORY—FROM MY PERSPECTIVE.

IN SHORT, MOM,

I love you.

AND HERE'S WHY.

When I
was small,
you were
my world.

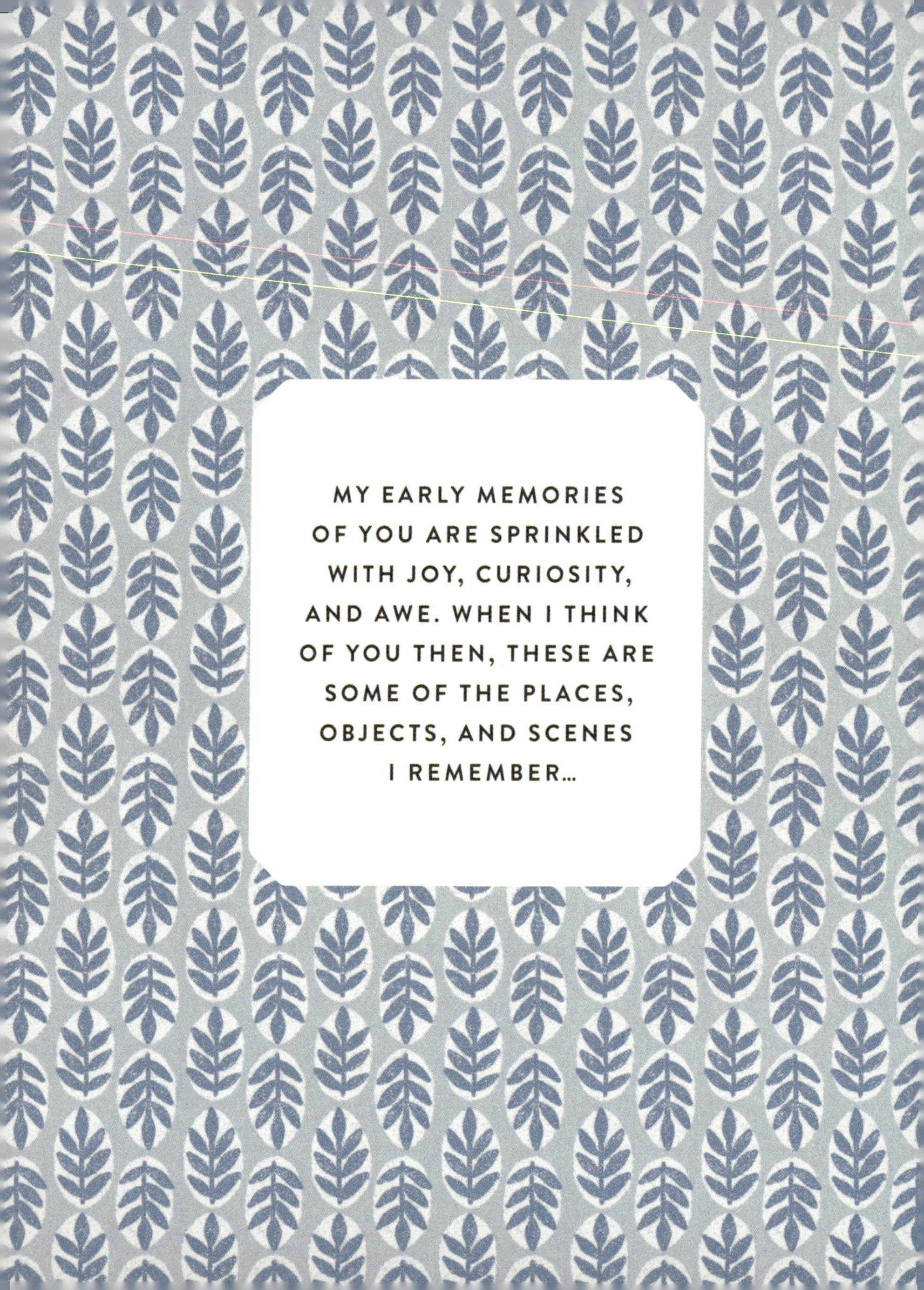
MY EARLY MEMORIES OF YOU ARE SPRINKLED WITH JOY, CURIOSITY, AND AWE. WHEN I THINK OF YOU THEN, THESE ARE SOME OF THE PLACES, OBJECTS, AND SCENES I REMEMBER…

IF YOU COULD SEE
YOURSELF BACK THEN
THE WAY I SAW YOU,
YOU'D SEE...

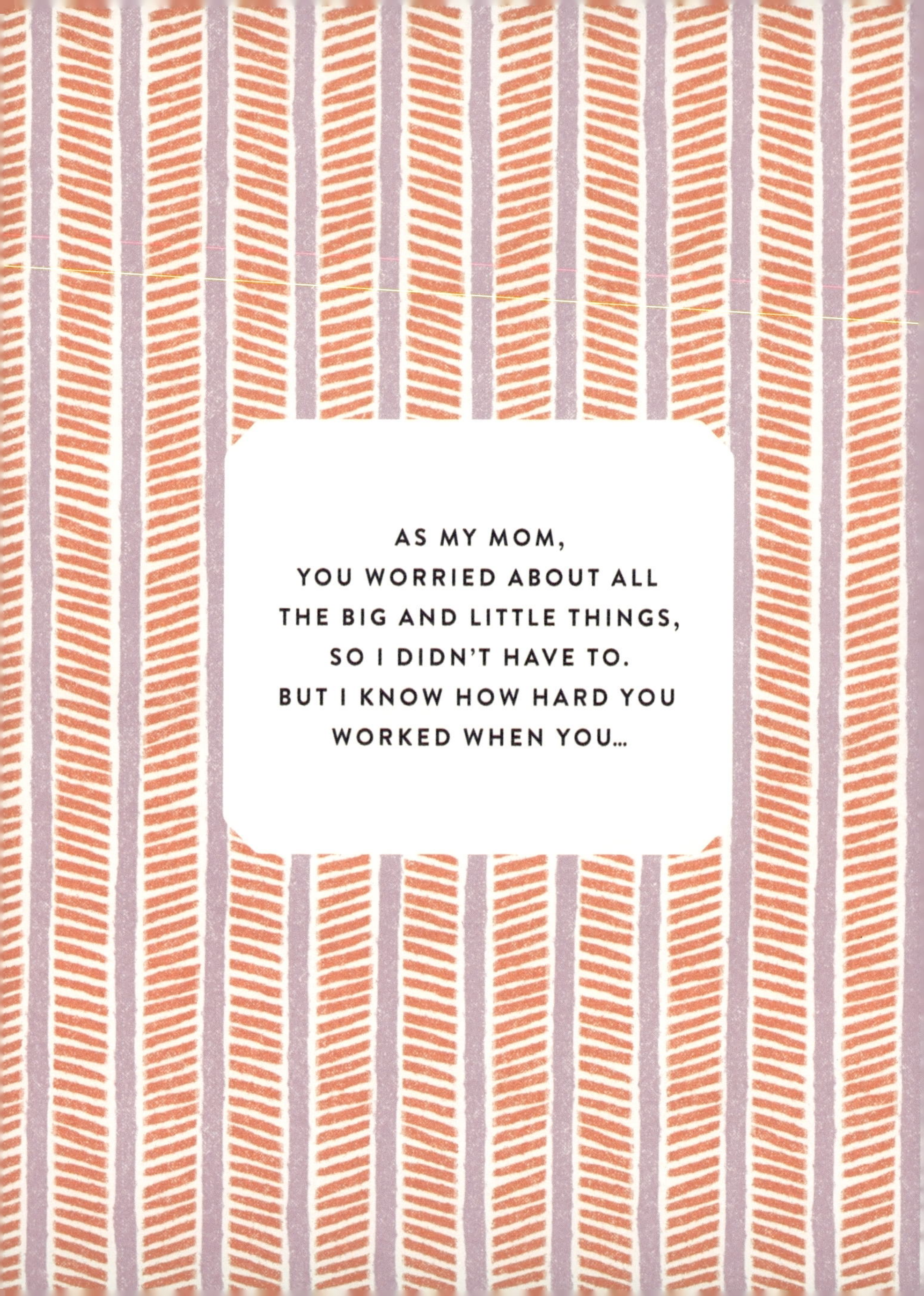
AS MY MOM,
YOU WORRIED ABOUT ALL
THE BIG AND LITTLE THINGS,
SO I DIDN'T HAVE TO.
BUT I KNOW HOW HARD YOU
WORKED WHEN YOU...

YOU MIGHT NOT REMEMBER,
BUT I'LL NEVER FORGET THE
WAY YOU MADE ME FEEL WHEN...

You were
my first model
for what is right,
what is good, and
what should be.

THE WORDS I WOULD CHOOSE ABOVE ALL OTHERS TO DESCRIBE YOU ARE…

THESE QUALITIES SHINE THROUGH THE MOST WHEN YOU'RE DOING THE THINGS YOU LOVE, AND THE THINGS YOU'RE SO GOOD AT, LIKE…

THERE ARE A FEW LESSONS THAT
YOU TAUGHT ME AT A YOUNG AGE,
MAYBE WITHOUT EVEN REALIZING IT.
YOU SHOWED ME THE WAY THEN,
JUST AS YOU DO TODAY.

BECAUSE OF YOU, I…

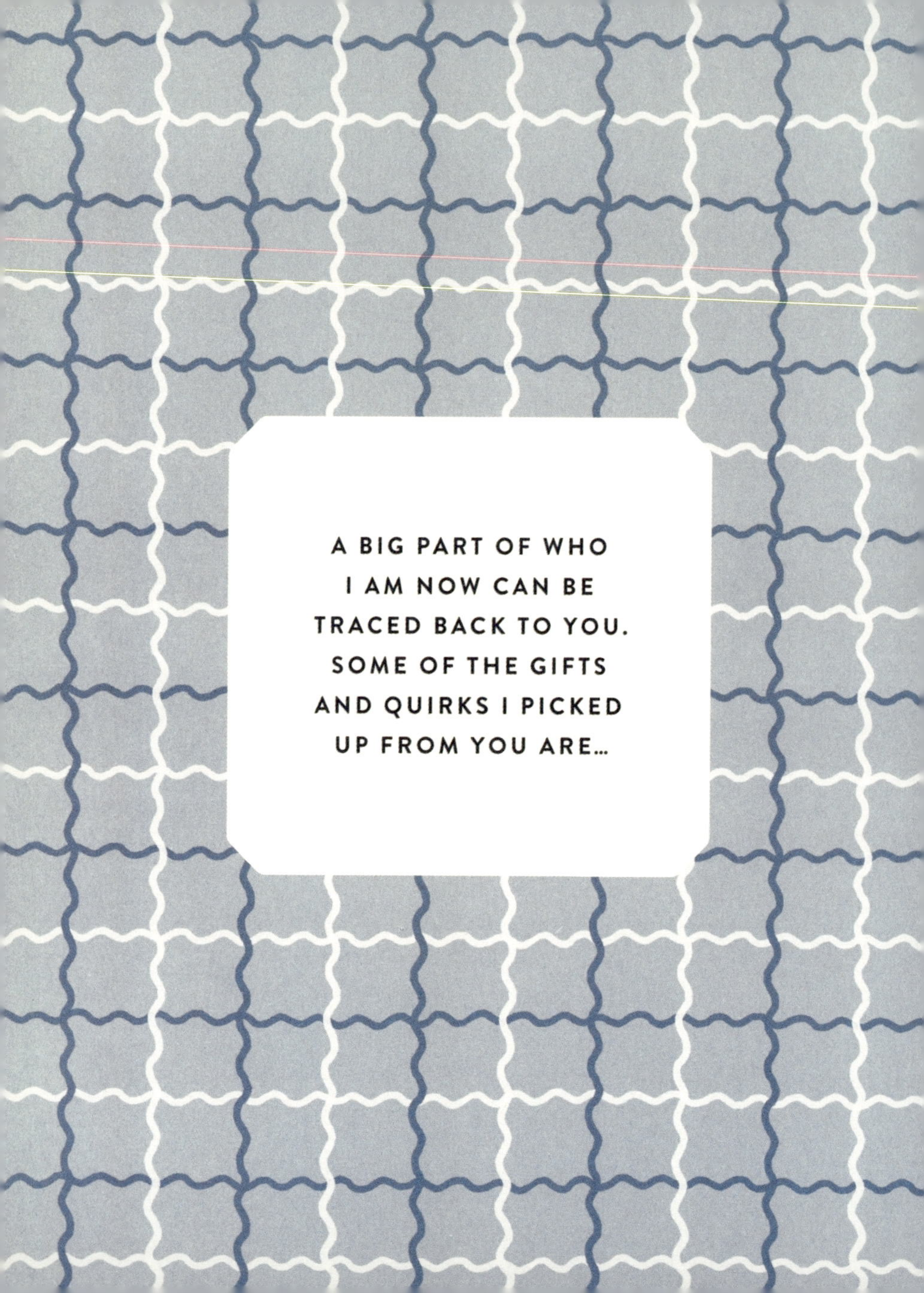

A BIG PART OF WHO I AM NOW CAN BE TRACED BACK TO YOU. SOME OF THE GIFTS AND QUIRKS I PICKED UP FROM YOU ARE…

I HOPE I MAKE
YOU PROUD, LIKE YOU
MAKE ME. I'M FOREVER
AMAZED BY HOW YOU...

With you,
everyday moments
become golden
memories.

WHEN I WAS A KID,
YOU WERE JUST MY MOM.
AS I GREW, I GOT TO
KNOW YOU AS A WHOLE
PERSON AND CONNECTED
WITH YOU IN NEW WAYS.

I'LL NEVER FORGET THE TIME...

THE ROUTINES AND TRADITIONS YOU MADE FOR US HELPED SHAPE AND COLOR OUR DAYS TOGETHER. THESE ARE SOME OF MY FAVORITES...

AND A FEW TRADITIONS I HOPE TO CARRY ON…

SOMETIMES IT WAS WHEN
THINGS FELL APART
THAT WE REALLY CAME
TOGETHER (OR AT LEAST
HAD A GOOD LAUGH).

REMEMBER WHEN...

AT THE END OF THE DAY,
WHAT MATTERS MOST ARE
THE MOMENTS WE'VE SHARED.
OF ALL THE WAYS WE'VE
SPENT TIME TOGETHER,
THESE ARE THE MOST
SPECIAL TO ME…

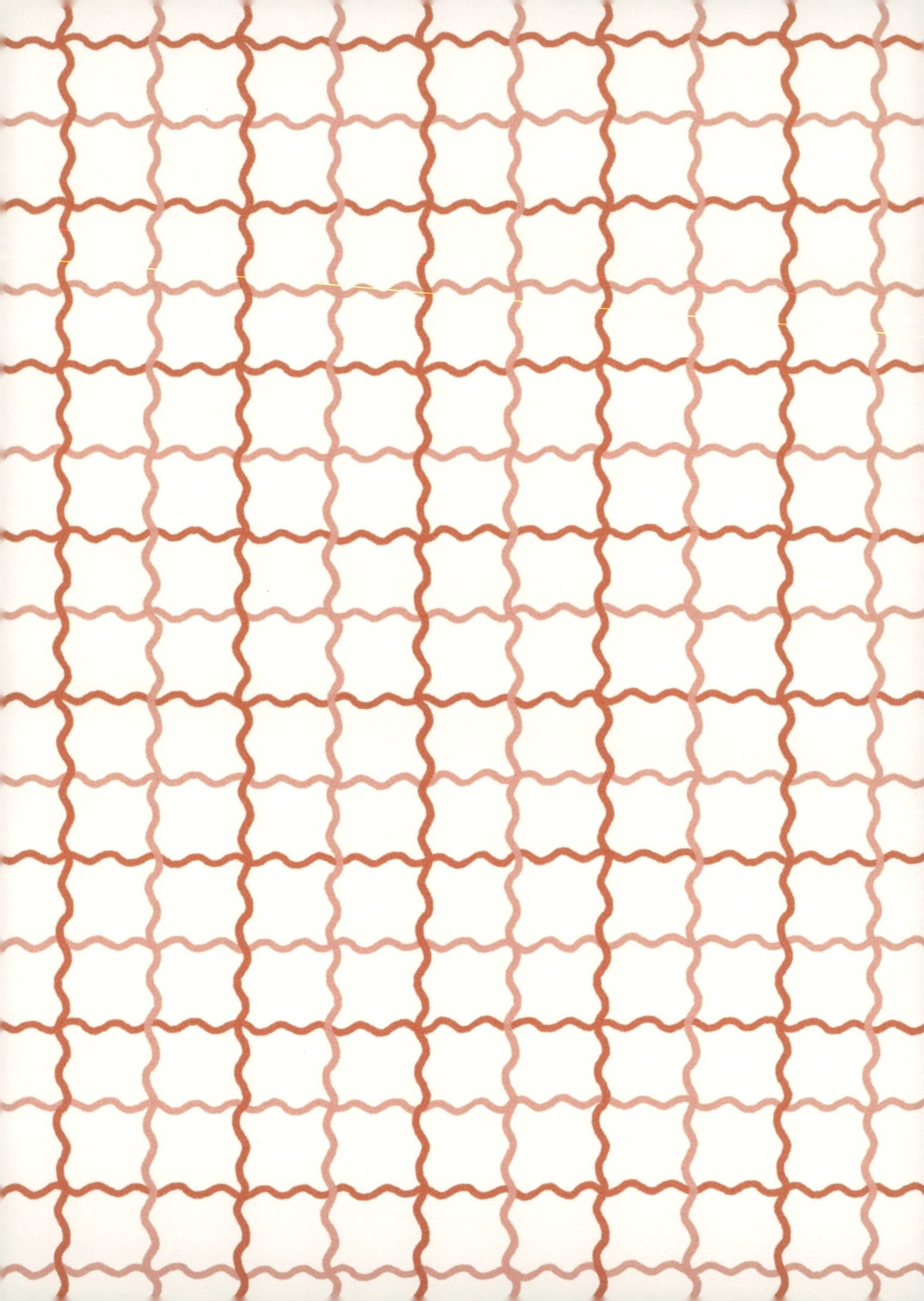

You're my home—
a place I know
I can always
come back to.

WHEN I WAS A KID, YOU DID SO MUCH FOR ME, LIKE…

AS I GOT OLDER, YOU CONTINUED TO WRAP ME IN THE BLANKET OF YOUR SUPPORT BY…

YOU'VE ALWAYS BEEN THERE
FOR ME—THROUGH MY MANY
PHASES, NOT-SO-BRIGHT IDEAS,
LITTLE SETBACKS, AND BIG WINS.

NOT JUST ANY MOM WOULD...

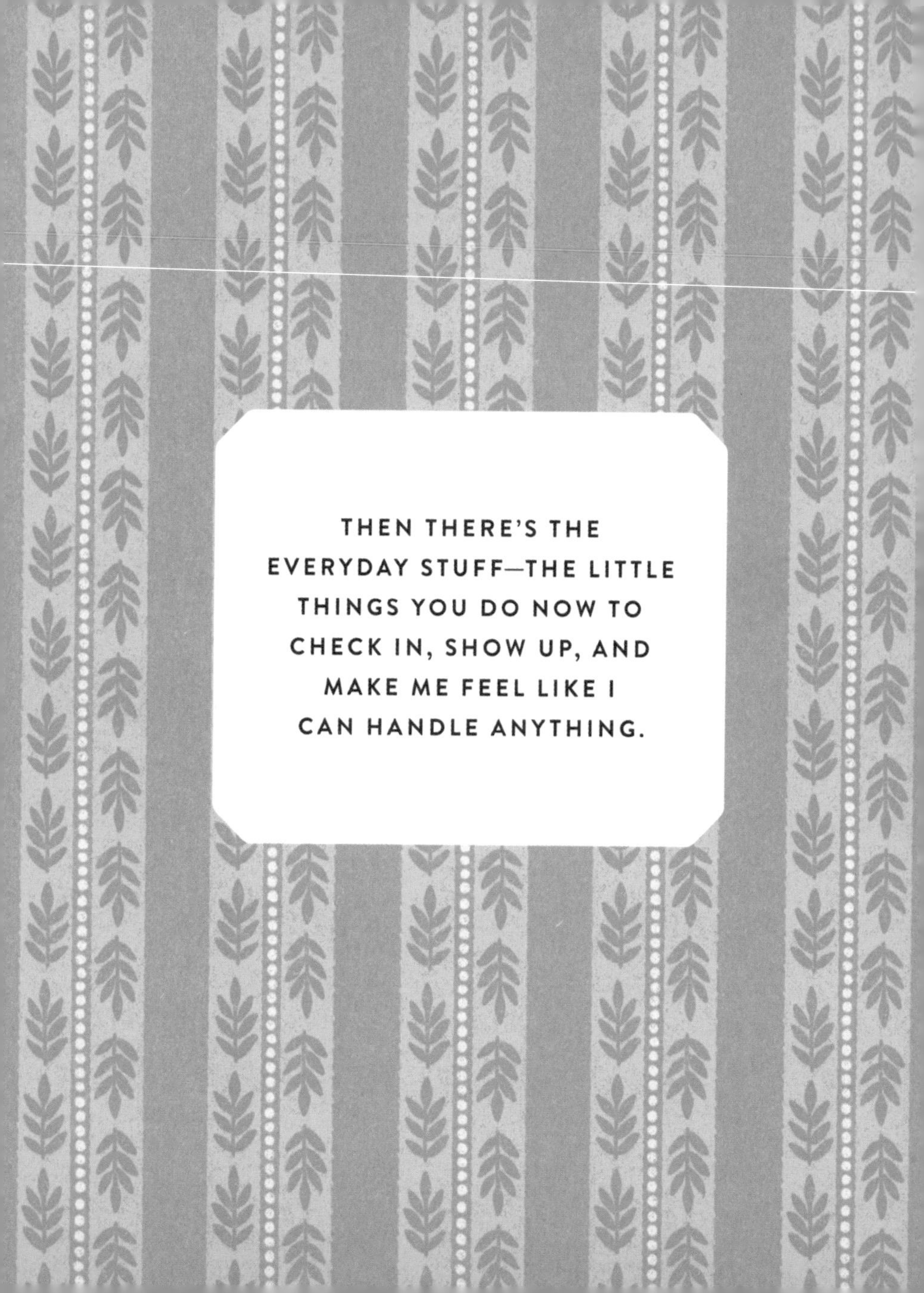
THEN THERE'S THE
EVERYDAY STUFF—THE LITTLE
THINGS YOU DO NOW TO
CHECK IN, SHOW UP, AND
MAKE ME FEEL LIKE I
CAN HANDLE ANYTHING.

THINGS LIKE...

I MAY NO LONGER NEED YOU
THE WAY I USED TO WHEN I WAS SMALL,
WHEN YOU INTRODUCED ME TO
THE WORLD WITH MY HAND IN YOURS.
BUT I KNOW YOUR HAND IS STILL
THERE IF I EVER NEED IT, LIKE WHEN...

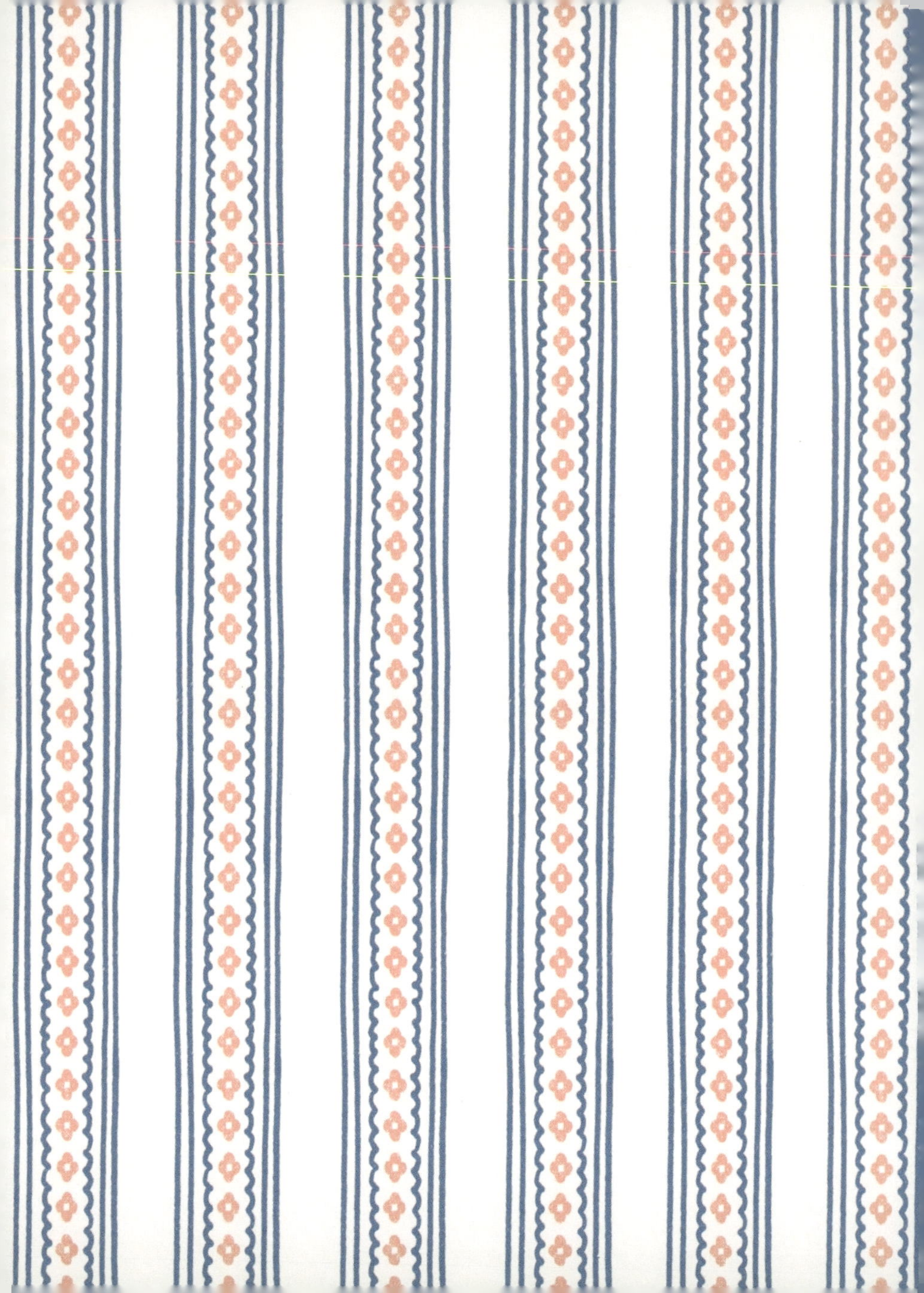

Our movie isn't over yet—our story grows every time we connect.

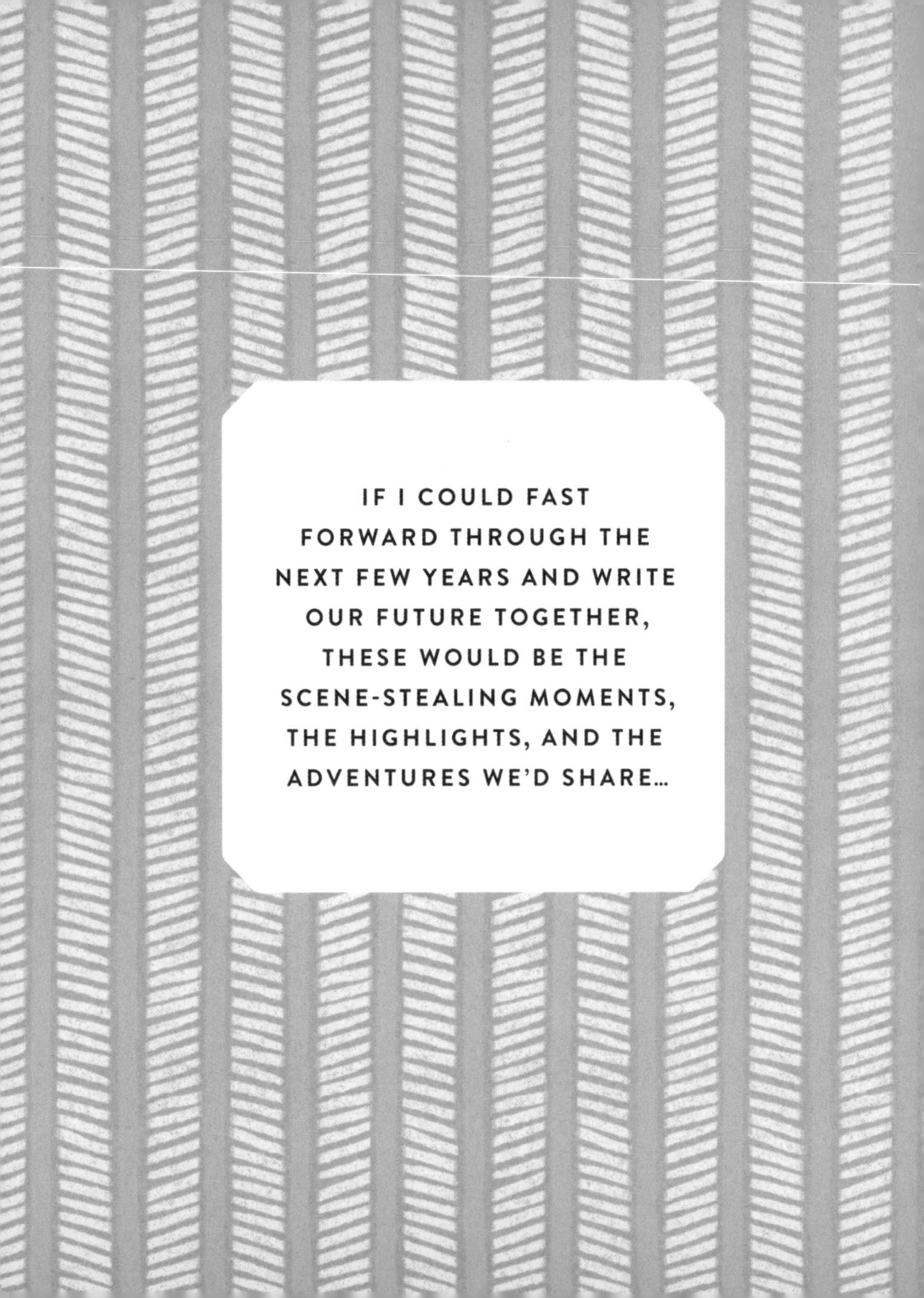

IF I COULD FAST FORWARD THROUGH THE NEXT FEW YEARS AND WRITE OUR FUTURE TOGETHER, THESE WOULD BE THE SCENE-STEALING MOMENTS, THE HIGHLIGHTS, AND THE ADVENTURES WE'D SHARE...

IF I COULD REWIND AND
RELIVE A DAY, MOMENT,
OR TIME OF LIFE WITH YOU,
IT WOULD BE WHEN...

BECAUSE OF YOU,
I GREW UP IN A
WORLD FULL OF…

IN LARGE PART
THANKS TO YOU,
I'M NOW...

Mom,
I hope you know...

____

____

____

____

____

____

...and never forget it.

An imprint of the Crown Publishing Group
A division of Penguin Random House LLC
1745 Broadway, New York, NY 10019
live-inspired.com | penguinrandomhouse.com

Copyright © 2026 by Compendium
Penguin Random House values and supports copyright. Copyright fuels creativity, encourages diverse voices, promotes free speech, and creates a vibrant culture. Thank you for buying an authorized edition of this book and for complying with copyright laws by not reproducing, scanning, or distributing any part of it in any form without permission. You are supporting writers and allowing Penguin Random House to continue to publish books for every reader. Please note that no part of this book may be used or reproduced in any manner for the purpose of training artificial intelligence technologies or systems.

Compendium and the Compendium colophon are registered trademarks of Penguin Random House LLC.

ISBN: 978-1-957891-67-5

Writer: Danielle Leduc McQueen
Designer: Jessica Phoenix
Editor: Bailey Vega
Production Manager: Shannon Lery

1st printing. Manufactured in China with soy inks on FSC®-Mix certified paper.

The authorized representative in the EU for product safety and compliance is Penguin Random House Ireland, Morrison Chambers, 32 Nassau Street, Dublin D02 YH68, Ireland, https://eu-contact.penguin.ie.

Create meaningful moments with gifts that inspire.

CONNECT WITH US
live-inspired.com | sayhello@compendiuminc.com

@compendiumliveinspired
#compendiumliveinspired